WHEATLEY, B......
HERO

CENTRAL LI
ALBION S

PLA   HCL

ALS No. B38 473 4654

This item should be returned on or before the last date stamped above. If not in demand it may be renewed for a further period by personal application, by telephone, or in writing. The author, title, above number and date due back should be quoted.   LS/3

British Library Cataloguing in Publication Data.
A catalogue record for this book is available from the British Library.

First published 2001

© 2001 Barrie Wheatley
All photographs © 2001 respective owners as indicated

Published by Kingston Press

All rights reserved. No part of this publication may be reproduced, stored in a retrieval system, or transmitted, in any form, or by any means, electronic, mechanical, photocopying, recording, or otherwise, without prior written permission of the publishers.
This book is sold subject to the condition that it shall not, by way of trade or otherwise, be lent, resold, hired or otherwise circulated, in any form of binding or cover other than that in which it is published, without the publisher's prior consent.
The Author asserts his moral right to be identified as the Author of the work in accordance with the Copyright Design and Patents Act 1988.

ISBN 1 902039 11 4

Kingston Press is the publishing imprint of Kingston upon Hull City Libraries, Central Library, Albion Street, Kingston upon Hull, England HU1 3TF
Telephone: +44 (0) 1482 616814
Fax: +44 (0) 1482 616827
E-mail: kingstonpress@hullcc.demon.co.uk
Internet: www.hullcc.gov.uk/kingstonpress

Printed by Kingston upon Hull City Council Printing Services, 33 Witham, Kingston upon Hull, England HU9 1DA.

Introduction

_H__ERO_ was inspired by the biography, *Dan Billany: Hull's Lost Hero*, by Valerie A. Reeves and Valerie Showan. Their biography was the result of a lifetime's interest, which started after they read Billany's first book, *The Magic Door*, when they were young girls. A review of their biography in the Independent said: *"Such vital provincial histories challenge the contempt with which our current political culture regards local politics and history. The local and the modern have been seen as incompatible in the rhetoric of both Thatcher and Blair. In the coming debate about a more inclusive definition of Englishness, voices such as Billany's - and biographies and local histories such as this - are likely to be critical."*

The passion with which Reeves and Showan wrote about Dan Billany's life and work inevitably rubbed off on me. After reading their biography I felt that I wanted to know more about this man who had dragged himself up from an impoverished working class background, who had a passion for Romantic poetry, left-wing politics and social justice and who spent his short life looking for the truth about himself and the world about him. His ability to face up to his homosexuality, given the social and moral constraints of his time, showed how brave and honest he was and how he must have struggled inwardly towards acceptance of his sexuality against all the odds.

Valerie Reeves and Val Showan were a great help to me in the search for more information about Dan Billany's life. They loaned me original manuscripts and their own treasured copies of Billany's books. As I read through these manuscripts and read and re-read the books I could see the promise in Billany that had been cut short. The voice, which spoke through the books, seemed alive and contemporary. All the works are full of finely drawn characterisation and acute observation and Billany's honesty, integrity and humour shines through in every page. Billany's book

The Opera House Murders was published by Faber when he was twenty seven and it secured the keen interest of T. S. Eliot, who saw a stellar career in the making. After writing this first novel, Billany was called up for active service and left England in February 1942 for Egypt. He was captured and put into an Italian P.O.W. camp. *The Trap* and *The Cage* were both written inside the camp and were published posthumously. Of all the books to emerge from the Second World War, they are still regarded as the most original. *The Trap* is frequently reprinted and has been translated into many languages. *The Cage* was co-written with David Dowie, the fellow prisoner of war with whom Billany fell hopelessly and unrequitedly in love. The manuscripts of *The Trap* and *The Cage*, written in thirteen exercise books and left for safe keeping with an Italian family, were posted back to Billany's family after the war. I have drawn on *The Cage* extensively in **HERO**.

David Dowie and Dan Billany went on the run together after escaping during the Italian armistice of August 1943. **HERO** is set in November 1943 in the mountains east of Rome, their last known point of contact before they disappeared without trace. The play tells the story of Dan's relationship with David Dowie and their struggle to come to terms with what was happening to them, set against the background of Dan's past life.

Barrie Wheatley
July 2001

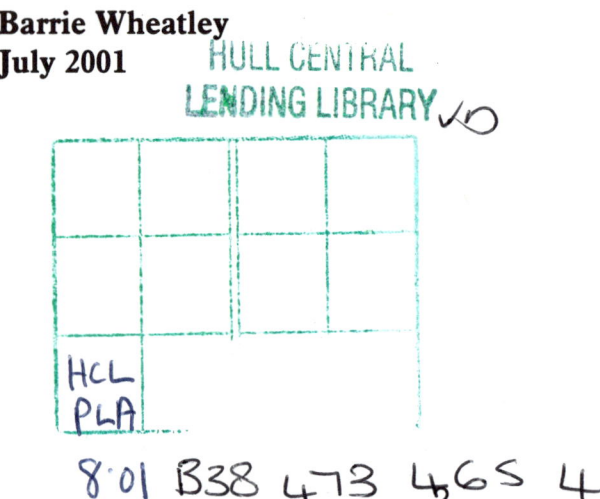

Cast list

HERO was first performed at Hull Screen Library Theatre in July 2001 after a preview at Northern Theatre Company's Studio Two in Hessle Road, Hull, with the following cast:

Arturo	Chris Gruca
Alec	James Chubb
David Dowie	Richard Healy
Dan Billany	Danny Sproats
Leo Peters	James Chubb
Jack Crossley	Matthew Stathers
Miss Trippitt	Katy Burgess
Dorothy Warner	Kirsty Applegarth
Joan Billany	Katy Burgess
Bill	Chris Gruca
Alan Matsen	Matthew Stathers
Henry	James Chubb

All other parts are played by members of the cast

Directed by	Barrie Wheatley
Set Design	Bryan Williams
Costumes	Vicky Reynolds
Stage Manager	Marcus Heald

The production at Hill Street Theatre, Edinburgh as part of the Edinburgh Festival Fringe, from August 3rd to August 14th 2001 is with the same cast.

Please note: This text preceeded the first production. Changes may have been made in rehearsal.

All applications to perform this play should be made to Kingston Press, Hull Central Library, Albion Street, Kingston Upon Hull, HU1 3TF. Telephone (01482) 616814, fax (01482) 616827, e-mail kpress@hullcc.demon.co.uk

About the writer

This is Wheatley's eighth play. Previous work, all performed by Northern Theatre Company, includes: *Do You Love Me?*, *First Aid*, *Family Values*, *Car Boot Sunday*, *Blue Skies*, *Taking Care of Fred and Ginger* and *Dancin' in Line*.

First Aid, *Family Values* and *Blue Skies* were performed at the Edinburgh Fringe. *Blue Skies* was toured as part of the Library Service's National Year of Reading Project. *Dancin' in Line* recently completed a successful tour of the Yorkshire and Lincolnshire region and earned much needed money for Northern Theatre Company's School of Performing Arts Roof Appeal.

He has written for Theatre in Education and his play *Talking to Lisa* was toured in conjunction with the East Riding Health Authority and Hull University and made into a video.

Wheatley works as a lecturer with students who are visually impaired at Hull College and founded the Access Centre Theatre Company, a theatre workshop for students with disabilities, which has performed throughout the region.

About the cast

Danny Sproats teaches English at South Holderness School. Last year he appeared at the Fringe in the successful Tom Lehrer review, *Poisoning the Pigeons in the Park*, and *The Gasman Cometh*, the sell-out Flanders and Swann review. He played the lead in Ayckbourn's *Gizmo* which was performed at the National Theatre as part of the BT Connections competition. He is reviving his role in *The Gasman Cometh* this year at the Gilded Balloon.

Richard Healey is studying computer technology at Humberside University and this is his first time at the Fringe. He comes from Ruislip in Middlesex and was a member of the Beck Youth Theatre, where he played in various productions including *Guys and Dolls* as Sky Masterson; *Carousel*; *The Lion, the Witch and the Wardrobe*; and *Pirates of Penzance* as The Major General. He has appeared in several TV commercials.

Chris Gruca is originally from Iowa, USA, and is a lecturer in performing arts at Wyke College, Hull. He has appeared at the Edinburgh Fringe in *Assassins* as John Wilkes Booth; *Pacific Overtures* as The Shogun's Mother and the American Admiral; *Unidentified Human Remains and the True Nature of Love* as David; *Blue Skies* as John and last year's NTC production of *Cocktales*, at Hill Street Theatre, as Phil.

James Chubb works for Ideal Standard in Hull and is currently on a teacher course at Hull College. Originally from Sheffield and a graduate of the University of Derby, his theatre experience includes: the part of Oedipus in *Oedipus the King* and Jesus in *Jesus Christ Superstar*.

Kirsty Applegarth works for Kingston Communications in Hull. Kirsty has appeared at the Fringe in *Love Kevin* (later performed at the National Theatre), *The Rink*, *Myra and Me* and *Blue Skies*. She has toured in cabaret and appeared in a variety of roles in productions for NTC since completing a performing arts course at Wyke College.

Katy Burgess is a student of performing arts at Wyke College. She has appeared in *Saved*, *Blood Wedding*, *Follies* and *Jungle Book* and is taking a year out before auditioning for drama schools.

Matthew Stathers is appearing at the Fringe for the first time. He is studying Performing Arts at Wyke College, where he has recently completed a tour of Germany with *A Slice of Saturday Night*. Next year he auditions for Drama School.

Bryan Williams is an artistic director of NTC and a lecturer in Spatial and TV and Theatre Design at Hull College. His design for the musical play *Sanctus* (performed by NTC at Queen Elizabeth Hall, London) was selected for exhibition by the Society of British Theatre Designers.

Marcus Heald has worked as stage manager for NTC for ten years, both at Studio Two and other venues in the region such as Hull Truck and Hull New Theatre. He has worked at the National Theatre on the occasions when NTC has been invited to perform there. He has toured extensively with both NTC and the Leap Dance Company and stage managed for NTC at several venues on the Fringe. He recently had his legs waxed to raise funds for the NTC Roof Appeal - there's dedication for you!

About Northern Theatre Company

Northern Theatre Company was founded by Richard Green and Bryan Williams twenty-five years ago. The company performs at several venues in Hull as well as at their own Studio Two Theatre in Hessle Road.

The Hessle Road premises house a busy and prestigious school of performing arts, where local talent is carefully nourished. Many ex students are currently employed in the professional theatre, some at this moment appearing in West End productions.

It is a fortunate coincidence that Dan Billany, the subject of **HERO**, was born and brought up in Hessle Road, not five minutes away from NTC's theatre and school. Dan Billany would have been proud to see lads and lasses from his home area being given the opportunity to express their natural talents and to better themselves.

Northern Theatre Company has gained a reputation over the years at the Edinburgh Fringe with acclaimed productions such as *Assassins* and *Pacific Overtures* (five stars) as well as with original cutting edge pieces such as Richard Green's own *Love Kevin*. Last year's productions of *The Gas Man Cometh* and *Poisoning the Pigeons in the Park* played to sell out audiences and Green's play, *Cocktales* attracted audiences that were used to more controversial drama. At the 2000 Fringe Festival, NTC was one of the top six best selling companies. In 2001, as well as Wheatley's play **HERO**, NTC is bringing *The Gas Man Cometh* back to the Fringe, along with *Mad Dogs and Englishmen*, a new review based on the work of Noel Coward.

NTC is always pleased to support new writing and has performed many original pieces at the Fringe in the past, including several well received plays by the author of **HERO**.

Photographic extracts from the book - Dan Billany, Hull's Lost Hero

Dan Billany (1940).
©Jerome of Hull.

A typical snap of Dan during his student years taken with Joan's box camera showing him reading on the couch at Lakeside Grove.
©Kingston Press

During his imprisonment Dan developed a talent for drawing portraits. Here is his pencil sketch of David Dowie with inset photograph of David.
© Kingston Press
Photograph: ©Imperial War Museum

Two of Dan's sketches to illustrate the manuscript of The Cage. Both show life in the prisoner-of-war camp at Capua. Right, Hut 1, whose inmates described themselves as "round the bend" or "bag-happy".
©Kingston Press

The Syndicate. This was a group of five prisoners formed for the purpose of sharing parcels of Red Cross food, which they cooked on improvised stoves.
© Kingston Press

Members of the cast in rehearsal

Chris Gruca, Mathew Stathers, Kirsty Applegarth, Danny Sproats
© Northern Theatre Company

Danny Sproats, Richard Healy
© Northern Theatre Company

Kirsty Applegarth, Richard Healy, Chris Gruca, Mathew Stathers,
© Northern Theatre Company

Danny Sproates, Mathew Stathers, Richard Healy
© Northern Theatre Company

HERO

by Barrie Wheatley

(Inspired by the biography *Dan Billany, Hull's Lost Hero*
by Valerie A. Reeves and Valeric Showan, Kingston Press 1999)

Nightfall on a November night in 1943 on the slopes of the Abruzzi mountains, east of Rome. The road to Rome lies below across a flat plain. South, beyond Naples, are the Allied lines.

On stage is a hut which is resting on a moveable truck. The roof, front and one side of the hut is cut away to reveal the interior. Inside the hut there is a bunk bed, a table, a chair and a stove. There are cooking utensils and some wood beside the stove. On the remaining wall is a small cupboard. On the table are tin plates, a couple of mugs and an oil lamp. The rest of the stage is empty except for a small rostrum. The SFX of a dog barking in the distance can be heard as Alec Harding and Arturo enter.

ARTURO: Ecco la capanna.

Alec calls quietly off stage.

ALEC: Dan, David up here. We've found the hut.

David and Dan enter. David is supporting Dan, who is obviously ill and exhausted.

ARTURO: La porta non e chiusa.

Arturo has opened the door to the hut.

ALEC: Come on, old chap, you can get some rest now.

Alec helps David to support Dan and they enter the hut. Arturo shuts the door and lights the oil lamp. There is the sound of a whistle and a dog barking further off. Dan sits on the bunk bed.

ALEC: It sounds as if they're moving away.

DAVID: Do you think it would be safe to light the stove?

ALEC: E pericoloso accendere la stufa?

ARTURO: Si, e troppo rischioso.

ALEC: It's too risky.

DAVID: Let's have a look at you Dan.

David examines the dressing of a wound in Dan's upper left chest area.

DAVID: The bleeding seems to have stopped. How do you feel?

DAN: Cold.

Dan goes into a coughing spasm

DAVID: Here, put this round you. You're lucky. The bullet went clean through.

David puts some old sacking round Dan's shoulders.

ALEC: Are you going to be able to make it?

DAN: I need a rest, that's all.

DAVID: How much further do we have to go?

ALEC: Arturo says it's about a hundred and fifty kilometres to the Allied Lines. That's somewhere just north of Naples. Conditions are bad, there's a lot of snow on the high ground. The area is swarming with Germans.

ARTURO: Dan non sembra bene. Voi siete pazzi da continuare. Dovete andare a Roma. Mio cugino vi nascondera. Sarete sicuri. Ci sono centinaia di prigionieri di guerra nascosti la. Roma sara liberata primo di Natale.

DAVID: What?

ALEC: He says we are mad to go on. He wants us to go to Rome. He has a cousin who will hide us. There are hundreds of POW's there. He says Rome will be liberated by Christmas.

DAVID: Maybe we should do that.

ARTURO: Si. Mio cugino ha un grande appartamento sulla Via dei Farnesi. Il suo nome e Enrico. Lui conosce i movimenti della Resistenza.

ALEC: His cousin, Enrico, has an apartment on the Via dei Farnesi. He's in contact with the Resistance. But I don't like the idea of Rome. I think we should carry on to the front.

DAVID: Yes. I think so too. Look, why don't you and Arturo go on and meet the contact. You can get some help and come back for us.

ALEC: OK. That makes sense. *To Arturo*. Noi due andremo avanti.

Arturo shrugs and puts his rucksack on the table.

ARTURO: Wine. Food.

Arturo goes over to Dan and hugs him and kisses him on both cheeks.

ARTURO: Arrivederci, Dan.

DAN: Thank you, Arturo. Arrivederci.

Arturo goes to hug and kiss David but David offers his hand.

ARTURO: *Laughing.* Ah, yes. No touch - inglese

They shake hands.

DAVID: Goodbye. Take care, Alec.

ALEC: We'll be back before you know it. Keep warm.

David turns down the lamp as Arturo and Alec exit. He looks out of the door.

DAVID: It's starting to snow. The weather changes so quickly in the mountains.

David shuts the door and turns up the lamp. He examines the contents of the rucksack.

DAVID: Do you want something to eat? There's some polenta and bread and cheese.

DAN: Save it till later. I wouldn't mind a drink though.

David takes a bottle of wine from the rucksack.

DAVID: You mean this kind of drink?

Dan nods and David wipes a couple of mugs and pours the wine.

DAN: The Italians are such good people. Dino and his family have shared everything they have with us.

DAVID: I'll never understand why they want to be so helpful. They could have been shot by the Germans for hiding us.

DAN: It's called the goodness of human nature.

DAVID: Not a lot of that around these days.

DAN: Stop being a cynical old fart. It doesn't become you.

Dan has a coughing spasm. He holds his chest in pain.

DAVID: Are you all right?

DAN: It's not the cough that carries you off,
It's the coffin they carry you off in.

DAVID: Maybe you should lie down and try to get some sleep.

DAN: I don't want to sleep.

He looks at David.

Give me another drink.

David pours more wine and then goes to peep through the door.

DAVID: God. It's snowing like mad.

Dan has a coughing spasm.

DAN: I'm cold.

David sits next to Dan and pulls the sacking more closely around him.

DAN: Listen how quiet it is. Do you realise that this is the first time we've ever really been alone together. There was never a time in all the prison camps when there wasn't somebody around.

As David tries to make Dan more comfortable, Dan places his hand on top of David's hand.

DAVID: I'm going to light the fire.

He gets up and goes to the stove.

DAN: It's not safe.

DAVID: Nobody will see the smoke in this weather. You can't see your hand in front of your face out there.

David starts to build the fire. Dan looks at him smiling. He laughs.

DAVID: What?

DAN: Arturo is right. No touch - English.

DAVID: That's the way I've been brought up.

DAN: I know. Stiff upper lip, lads. Bulldog Drummond rules, eh?

> Never let anyone see what you're really feeling.
> God, all that pretence seems so unnecessary now.

Dan takes two cigarettes out of a packet, lights them both and offers one to David. Dan smiles as he sees David cringe.

DAN: Don't look so put out. There's no one around to see here.

DAVID: You remind me of Bette Davis when you do that.

DAN: Bette Davis? Isn't she terrific?

Dan does an impression of Bette Davis. David grins wryly.

DAN: Maybe she could play the lead in my film. The Yanks have published my book, you know. They were negotiating the film rights. Have you ever heard of Ed Fitzgerald?

DAVID: No.

DAN: He broadcasts on American radio. He said: *American accent.* "The kid has got it." That's me. "I'm breaking the rules and rating "It Takes a Thief" Grade double A. So don't grab the book today; get it within the hour."

DAVID: You're a good writer, Dan.

DAN: *American accent.* I know, kiddo. *Posh British accent.* The Times said, "Mr Billany is a first class, he-man, thriller writer." *Normal accent.* I love writing Robbie Duncan stories. He's everything I'm not, I suppose: confident, a man of action - a hero.

"Robbie Duncan, temporarily in residence at Granby House as tutor to Jack, battles his way through one tricky situation after another by a combination of fine brain and physical prowess." We could do with Robbie here now.

DAVID: Do you think the stuff we wrote in the camps will ever be published?

DAN: Sure thing, kiddo. Those two books are triple A material.

DAVID: It doesn't seem very likely: thirteen scruffy exercise books stuck up in Dino Meletti's loft with his chickens. We'll be lucky if we see them again.

DAN: Have faith, mio pocco pollo, Dino will take care of them. He promised to send them on to us after the war.

DAVID: And then you think they'll be published?

DAN: "The Trap" is the best thing I've ever written.

DAVID: What about our little joint venture?

DAN: That's got to be published, it tells everything. I'm not sure about the title, though: "For You the War Is Over".

DAVID: A bit too long?

DAN: A bit premature, maybe.

Dan takes a drink. He winces with pain. They are quiet for a moment.

DAN: Do you think it will ever be really over?

DAVID: We're nearly at the front. After that it's only a matter of...

DAN: Aren't you scared?

DAVID: Of what?

DAN: When it is all over, how can we go back to being what we were after all we've been through?

DAVID: Well, it will be difficult to settle down at first, I suppose, but we'll get back into our normal routines and...

DAN: No. I'm not going back. I'm going forward. *American accent.* And so, as the sun sets on this beautiful Italian landscape, our two intrepid heroes continue their gallant march towards the front. Onwards, ever onwards - to freedom! *Normal accent.* So, we get over the allied lines. The war finishes. We take our civvy suits out of the wardrobe, we marry our girls and live happily ever after.

DAVID: I don't think my civvy suit will fit me any more. I've outgrown it.

DAN: And what about your girl? Will she still fit you?

David looks at Dan for a long moment.

DAVID: Yes. I think she will.

Dan moves away and stands looking through a gap in the planks in the door.

DAN: Freedom. I've never felt freer than I do now. I wasn't free before the war. I felt trapped by everything around me. I wanted to change the world, but I should have been trying to change me.

There is the SFX of music - "The Red Flag" as the lights crossfade and come up on Leo Peters, who is standing on the rostrum addressing a small audience. Two men move the truck, turning it round so that the back of the hut is facing the audience. A poster on the wall says, "JOIN THE NATIONAL UNEMPLOYED WORKERS MOVEMENT". The two men join the small crowd.

PETERS: So you think Nationalisation will bring you freedom? It's got a fine ring to it, that word. But what will it mean to you, the working men and women, who form the backbone of this country? It's nothing but a conspiracy - a pact with Capitalism to oppress the workers still further. Our illustrious MP, Commander Kenworthy, would have us believe that it's all part of a socialist programme. Nonsense. State Capitalism - that's all it is. But, that's enough from me...

IST. HECKLER:
Aye, more than enough. Bloody rubbish you talk.

PETERS: Let me introduce our next speaker. Dan Billany. A true man of the people. Dan.

Dan enters from around the truck. He is dressed in civvy clothes. He stands on the rostrum.

DAN: They say that things are improving. Are they improving for you, or you? Have you got any more money in your pocket?

>Things might be improving down there, in Park Lane and Mayfair, but I don't see much improvement round here in the streets of Hull.

1ST HECKLER:
>There'd be a bloody big improvement round 'ere if you shut your gob.

DAN:
>That's what they'd like: for us all to shut our gobs and just sit back and accept things. While we're all shutting our gobs, people are being thrown out of work.

2ND HECKLER: *Positioned R of block.*
>I bet you've never had a bloody job. What are you a bloody college boy?

DAN:
>I go to the Technical College in Park Street.

1ST HECKLER:
>Ooh! Technical College.

2ND HECKLER:
>Bloody thought so. Bloody college boy.

DAN:
>But I've been in jobs - and out of jobs. I've been means tested and I've been refused the dole. The only reason I'm at College is because I'm on a free place for the unemployed.

1ST HECKLER:
>So who keeps you, then, your Daddy?

2ND HECKLER:
>I've never seen you before. I bet you're not from round here.

DAN: I was born in Hessle Road in a two up and two down, with the lavvy down the yard. I know what it's like to have a cold arse first thing in a morning.

WOMAN HECKLER: Aah! Come 'ere and let me rub it for you, love.

DAN: And my father's a tram conductor. He's one of the lucky ones, he's got a job now. But he's been on the dole half his working life, just like most of you.

2ND HECKLER: Anyway, you didn't ought to be 'ere. You ought to be in bloody Russia with all the rest of your Commy pals.

DAN: I'm a Socialist and an Internationalist. And I belong here just as much as you do.

1ST HECKLER: So, what would you do that this bloody hopeless lot in power can't do?

DAN: I tell you what I wouldn't do. I wouldn't sell out like Ramsey McDonald did. Yes, you Labour supporters can hang your heads in shame. What has he left us with, eh? Baldwin: besotted by Free Trade and the Gold Standard. Free Trade? How long must the working man be put out of work, have his wages squeezed down, be kept on the poverty line, so that some capitalist can ride around in a nice big car. Things are improving, they say. A million private cars, they say. Aye, and getting on three million unemployed.

But, in spite of all the troubles we have here, we must not turn our backs on what is happening in Europe. We cannot ignore the evils of Fascism. And it's already on our doorstep. Fifteen hundred people at a meeting at Leeds Town Hall with Moseley and his Blackshirts. Lord Rothermere's Daily Mail says, "Hurrah for the Blackshirts". God help us if they ever get a foothold over here.

The working class must stick together. Join your unions. If you're out of work, join the National Unemployed Workers Movement. Organise! Organise and fight! Fight for your freedom!

1ST HECKLER:
Piss off! You're all bloody mouth, like the rest. You lot spout hot air, while we live on bloody fresh air.

The meeting breaks up in disarray and the small crowd disperses. Dan and Leo try to hand out leaflets, then start packing up.

DAN: I lost them.

PETERS: You let it get personal.

DAN: They're so apathetic. Why don't they care?

PETERS: They don't have much to care about.

DAN: No, I suppose not.

PETERS: Cheer up! You can't win them all. Come on, I'll buy you a pint.

They go to exit.

DAN: I thought I'd better not tell them that we've moved to Gipsyville and we've got an inside lavvy now.

PETERS: Good job you didn't. They'd think you belonged to high society. Come on. There's always another day.

They exit behind the wall. Peters goes off. The two men enter and one carefully scrawls the word BOLLOCKS across the poster before they turn the truck and move it back to its original position as the lights cross fade.

DAN: We are killing a goose this Christmas,
The sweetest goose on earth;
Its cheeks are so grey and white, dear,
Its wings have been clipped from birth.

The goose is the Working Class, dear,
It has an elastic throat;
And it will swallow the *strangest* things,
As good little gooses ought.

I never really felt like one of them. I always seemed to be on the outside, looking in.

DAVID: That's what comes of being a writer and a poet.

DAN: A poet! Oh, aye!
Sung to the tune of the same name.
"Oh, for the wings, for the wings of a dove
And the dirty black arse of a crow.
I'd fly, oh so high, in the sky up above
And shit on the people below."

One of my more popular pieces. It went down well in Hessle Road in Hull. Hessle road! The smell of fish. Rows of two up and two down with a lavvy outside the back. Front steps scrubbed and scoured and everywhere a feeling of belonging. But if you love music and the theatre you don't belong; if you wear plus fours with fancy brogues you don't belong; if you read Wordsworth and Yeats and Auden in Hessle road...

Dan smiles and takes a drink.

DAVID: South East London's not much different from Hull, I guess, except for the smell of fish.

DAN: An' t'accent, lad.

DAVID: Yeah, and the accent, cock.

DAN: What about you, eh? Posh job in local government - town planning department, even. Studying to be an architect in a two up and two down with the lavvy down the back yard. You didn't exactly belong.

DAVID: Ah, but I learned to play rugger.

DAN: Bloody game! I was never any good at it. I had to get myself a sense of humour and a fountain pen.

DAVID: So, here we are stuck up the side of an Italian mountain. Two lads from the back streets who made good, eh? Lieutenant Billany, Sir!

David salutes.

DAN: Lieutenant Dowie, Sir.

Dan returns the salute.

Sung to the tune of "The Red Flag"

"The working class can kiss my arse,
I've got the foreman's job at last."

DAN: Here's to belonging.

They toast each other.

DAVID: Are you feeling warmer?

DAN: Yes, the wine helped.

DAVID: The fire's burning well, but the wood won't last the night. Let's hope Alec and Arturo get back soon.

They sit quietly for a moment looking at the stove.

DAN: David. Thanks.

DAVID: What for?

DAN: For being the only person who's ever tried to understand me.

DAVID: Hm. I don't know about that. I don't think I'll ever understand you.

DAN: You know what I mean. You make me feel that I - belong.

David looks at Dan then turns his attention back to the stove.

DAN: I know you hate it when I go on like this.

DAVID: Yes.

DAN: I'm sorry, but you know I've got to say what I feel.

DAVID: Unfortunately, yes.

DAN: I can't keep my mouth shut. But nobody will listen. That's why I write.

David moves away.

DAN: Anyway, I didn't "not belong" just because I preferred Beethoven to Bing. I never grew up. I was writing poems about love while the lads and lasses all around me were falling in love, getting married and having sex. Not necessarily in that order. Twenty three, twenty four and still a kid - still a virgin. When I started teaching, I didn't feel any different from the boys in my class who were twelve years younger than me.

DAVID: Maybe that's why you were such a good teacher.

DAN: I was a good teacher. I knew how to involve the kids and make them listen. I knew how to inspire them. Other teachers had given up on them. They were just working class layabouts who would never be anything more than factory fodder in their eyes. I knew those kids. I'd lived in the same street as most of 'em.

Dan smiles to himself. There is the SFX of a school bell and the hubbub of playground noise.

> The Magic Door. That's how I got the kids attention. That's how I taught History and Geography.

The lights dim and the hut revolves. On the wall is a blackboard. Several boys bring on benches and sit. The "boys" are adults dressed as twelve year olds. Dan comes forward as the lights come up.

BOYS: Me, Dan! Dan, it's my turn. Let me do it. Dan! Dan!

DAN: Alright, calm down. Jack, you do it.

Jack comes forward and draws a door on the blackboard.

BOYS: I could do better with my eyes shut. Where did you learn to draw, then, blind school? Rubbish! Come on hurry up.

Dan hands Jack an ornate silver door knocker, which Jack hangs on a nail in the blackboard in the middle of the door.

DAN: OK, Jack. Carry on.

Jack reads.

JACK: "Please, Sir" said Bartlett, "can't we go through the door today?"
"Hands up the boys who want to go through the door," said Mr. Billany. Of course every hand went up.

"All right," said Mr. Billany with a sigh. "I suppose I shall have to give in. "Crossley, do your stuff." Crossley banged the door knocker hard and the door opened.

A boy gets up and bangs the knocker on the blackboard as Jack says the line.

JACK: "Hello, folks," said the Winged Boy, flying out like a swallow and circling the classroom. He alighted on the gas bracket.
"No," shouted Mr. Billany "come off it, quick!" But it was too late. As soon as the Winged Boy put his weight on it, the gas bracket came down, bringing half the ceiling with it.
"You've done it now," said Mr. Billany to the Winged Boy. "You'd better get on mending that while we're gone, else there'll be a row."
With these words the great teacher strode through the Magic Door and the boys all strode after him. Mr. Billany sat down with a bump.
"Ow!" he said, "where am I?"
Then all the class fell on top of him.
"Ow!" said Mr. Billany again, with more feeling. They were in a long narrow ship manned by oarsmen.

The boys and Dan have moved the benches up against the rostrum into the shape of a ship. Dan stands on the rostrum and uses a window pole for the mast.

JACK: All the men were tall and broad with long fair hair. They wore helmets with two horns sticking forward which made them look rather savage. The sea was rough, the boat was rolling and pitching.

The boys and Dan mime the scene.

BOYS: *The boys sing.*
"Sons of the sea, bobbing up and down like this.
Sailing the ocean, bobbing up and down like this.
You can't beat the boys of the bulldog breed,
When they're bobbing up and down like this."

JACK: Mr. Billany, unable to stand, wrapped his arms fondly around the mast.
"How did you get here?" shouted the Captain.

DAN: M m m magic!

JACK: "Oh," said the Captain, "well maybe you can tell us the way to Britain."

DAN: I'm a stranger here myself: ask the boys.

BOY 1: Port your helm.

BOY 2: Hard a starboard.

BOY 3: Shiver your timbers.

BOY 4: Fasten your bootlaces.

BOY 1: Pull your socks up.

JACK: The Captain looked bewildered.
"I want to know where we are." he shouted.

DAN: All right. Don't shout. Where were you the last time you knew where you were?

JACK: "Jutland," said the Captain.

DAN: Jutland. Are you Jutes, then?

JACK: "I should think not," said the Captain. "We're Angles and proud of it."

BOY 1: Land - Ho!

DAN: That looks like Spurn Point.

JACK: "What's that?" asked the Captain.

DAN: That is the entrance to the river Humber.

BOYS: Good old Humber!

DAN: Now, it's no use looking for Hull, lads. It's all swampy land now. It won't be dry land until the river has changed its course and dykes have been built to keep the river in place.

JACK: The Angles and the boys all rowed madly.

BOYS: Heave! Heave!

JACK: Then suddenly they were high and dry on a sand bank.

The boys fall about. Dan still clings to the mast.

DAN: There's the river Hull. Look there's a wood with a village near it.

BOY 2: Ooh! Look. Britons.

BOY 3: Hey, them Britons wouldn't half be surprised if the New Holland Ferry boat came steaming over.

BOY 1: Let's take a Briton back with us.

BOY 2: You can't. He'd be locked up in prison. They don't have any clothes on. They've all got bare bums.

DAN: Look, lads, the Angles are creeping up on the Britons. Don't let them capture them. Shout a warning.

The scene erupts into noisy confusion. Dan stands holding onto the mast encouraging the boys as a stern faced MISS TRIPPITT enters. [Enter DSL]

MISS T: Mr. Billany!

The action stops. Dan turns to face Miss Trippitt still holding onto the mast.

DAN: Yes, Miss Trippitt. What can I do for you?

The low murmur of boys saying their seven times table can be heard off stage.

MISS T: I am trying to teach arithmetic next door.

DAN: So I hear.

MISS T: It is impossible with this cacophony [a harsh, discordant mixture of sounds] of noise in here.

BOY 1: Caca Caca Caca - ophony.

DAN: Shut up, Jim. Boys, it's time for your playtime.

BOY 1: Sorry, Dan.

The boys trudge off.

MISS T: Jim? Dan? Mr. Billany, when are you going to realize that the only way to educate these children is by disciplining them? You must create the proper environment for learning.

DAN: You can take a horse to water, Miss Trippitt, but you can't make it drink.

Move across to SR

MISS T: Chiltern Street School is not Summerhill. You may as well forget all you observed about teaching at that dreadful school.

DAN: I tell you what I observed at that "dreadful school". Children learn best when they are happy. We're training human beings, not automatons.

to weaken

MISS T: You are undermining the authority of all the staff. Once we lose authority, we have no hope of teaching anything.

DAN: Bugger authority.

MISS T: Well! I've had enough of this. I'm going to see the Head.

DAN: I'm sure he'll agree with every word you say, Miss Trippitt.

Exit

Miss Trippitt exits. Jack looks in.

JACK: Has the old battleaxe gone?

DAN: Now then, Jack. None of that. *Dan smiles.* Yes, she's gone.

The boys enter.

DAN: Right, lads. Sit on the floor, anywhere. We're going to do some poetry.

Dan hands Jack a book.

DAN: The poem Jack's going to read to us is a favourite of mine. It's a hard poem to understand, but I want you to listen and let the words flow over you. Try to find the music in the words. Some day, a long time from now, you may come across this poem and want to read it again and understand it. Page ninety three, Jack. I've marked the passage.

JACK: Intimations of Immortality from Recollections of Early Childhood by William Wordsworth.
"Our birth is but a sleep and a forgetting:
The soul that rises with us, our life's Star,
Hath had elsewhere its setting,
And cometh from afar:
Not in entire forgetfulness,
And not in utter nakedness,
But trailing clouds of glory do we come
From God, who is our home:
Heaven lies about us in our infancy!

The hut has been revolved and Dan is back inside. Spots pick out Dan and Jack.

JACK & DAN TOGETHER:
Shades of the prison house begin to close
Upon the growing Boy,

> But He beholds the light, and whence it flows,
> He sees it in his joy;
> The Youth, who daily farther from the east
> Must travel, still is Nature's Priest,
> And by the vision splendid
> Is on his way attended;

DAN: At length the man perceives it die away,
And fade into the light of common day.

The spot fades on Jack. The boys exit. The lights come up on the hut.

DAN: I did fall in love. Twice. The first time, I was nine or ten. She was a little brown haired girl with a blue dress, who lived in the next street. I called her Boadicca. The second time I was thirteen. His name was Joey. He had very fair hair and clear blue eyes and he was good and kind. Once, during the hot weather, we were walking home from school and he put his arm around my shoulders. My heart thumped so hard. I was scared to death that he would hear it. I never saw much of him after that. If we could only find our way back to the children we once were.

DAVID: Maybe some of us would prefer to forget all that.

DAN: What do you mean?

DAVID: Childhood. Most of us move on as quickly as we can.

David mends the fire. Dan coughs and winces with the pain.

DAN: I'm hungry.

David takes some bread and cheese out of the rucksack.

DAVID: Here.

DAN: Arturo's mamma makes good bread. It really fills you up, not like that soggy, pale stuff we get at home.

DAVID: Ah, but you couldn't make a decent bacon sandwich with this stuff. Give me a slice of mum's farmhouse loaf anytime.

DAN: It's one of the things I'll miss. As well as the old vino, of course. Any left?

David hands Dan the bottle.

DAVID: That's the last.

Dan pours himself a drink then pours a splash of wine onto the floor.

DAVID: What are you doing?

DAN: The last of the wine. I'm pouring a libation to the gods. You're supposed to make a wish.

DAVID: Oh, yes and what will you wish for?

DAN: You can't say, otherwise it won't come true.

DAVID: You just made all that up.

DAN: No. It was part of ancient Greek culture. They always made sure the gods were taken care of. They knew a thing or two, those Greeks.

DAVID: Well, I hope you get what you wished for.

DAN: Oh, I'm sure I will. Cin Cin!

Dan drains the mug.

DAN: This is a civilized drink.

DAVID: You seem to have acquired a taste for it.

DAN: It's rough and ready, but honest. It does just what it's supposed to do. No pretences. Just like the people here. Mil-le-graz-i-e.

Dan hands David the mug.

DAN: Won't you miss anything, David?

DAVID: I will miss some of the people. They've been good to us. People like Dino and his family and Arturo and his mamma. We owe them a lot. Maybe the government will cash the chitties we left them after the war.

DAN: Yes. It's a good life they lead: hard, but honest and good.

DAVID: Good enough, I suppose.

DAN: And they've got a healthy hatred of authority. They despise the pezzi grossi - the big pieces.

DAVID: That's why you get on so well with them.

DAN: I could live their kind of life.

DAVID: You talked about not belonging in Hessle Road. How do you think you'd fit in in Italy?

DAN: I feel I belong here.

DAVID: Why?

DAN: I suppose because in the last year everything that doesn't matter has been stripped away. Furniture and carpets and brick houses aren't life. Shops and trams and cars don't make civilization.

DAVID: Just put me on a tram with some money in my pocket going to the shops, that's civilization for me.

DAN: You know what I mean, David. We lived for months in Capua with just a pair of ragged shorts and a threadbare blanket, foraging in dustbins for food.

DAVID: You're going to tell me next that you miss the prison camps.

DAN: I do. It's funny isn't it?

DAVID: Bloody weird, if you ask me.

DAN: Come on, be honest. There was a strange kind of feeling of being liberated, wasn't there?

DAVID: Liberated?

DAN: A kind of limbo - no connection with the past or with the future. We had time.

DAVID: We had plenty of that. There was a freedom from responsibility, if that's what you mean. I enjoyed that. It was the first time in my life I could just think about myself. It was like being a kid again.

DAN: Yes. Exactly. Time to experiment. Time to be someone different if we wanted to.

DAVID: Do you remember when you shaved your head?

DAN: My god, yes.

DAVID: There were three of you did it. Silly buggers.

DAN: Mohawk, Kittyhawk and...

DAVID: Shitehawk.

Dan rubs his head.

DAVID: It looked like a bladder.

DAN: A haggis.

DAVID: An igloo.

DAN: Moby Dick.

DAVID: A stout lady swimming under water.

DAN: It attracted flies. I learned a lot about myself in that place.

DAVID: We all did.

Dan takes some polenta out of the rucksack.

41

DAN: Want some polenta?

DAVID: ~~I never thought I'd get to~~ No Thanks - don't like this stuff.

[handwritten: "No Thanks - don't" replacing "I never thought I'd get to"]

DAN: It's an acquired taste.

DAVID: I suppose you can get used to anything in time. But, don't get too used to it all, Dan. We'll be back home soon and all this will be just a memory.

DAN: Everything back home seems just a memory. Here seems more real than Hull or Pwllheli or *(SFX of Caruso singing)* gooseberry fool.

DAVID: Gooseberry fool?

DAN: Yes. That is an acquired taste.

*The lights dim and cross fade to a rug with a picnic basket on it. The area represents a field near **Dorothy Warner**'s house. Dorothy is putting food onto plates as she listens to a wind up gramophone playing Caruso singing Brindisi, Libiamo from La Traviata. Dan steps forward and joins her. He is wearing a sleeveless undervest.*

DAN: What is that stuff?

DOROTHY: Gooseberry fool.

DAN: No need to be personal. I've never tasted that before.

DOROTHY: There's a first time for everything.

DAN: Trifle, with little chocolate bits on top, that's what Mam used to make for Sunday afternoon tea.

DOROTHY: You mean vermicelli.

DAN: Vermicelli?

DOROTHY: It's Italian for little worms.

DAN: Yuck! All those years studying Latin and I never knew what vermicelli meant. That's what becomes of having a deprived childhood.

DOROTHY: You weren't deprived of very much.

DAN: Well, we certainly didn't live in a big house like yours. Look at all those chimney pots.

DOROTHY: It's only rented.

DAN: Fancy name and all. "Ty-Du". I used to deliver groceries on my bike to posh people like you.

DOROTHY: Did you? Oh, bless you. I hope they tipped you well.

DAN: No, they didn't as a matter of fact.

DOROTHY: Don't! You're bringing the tears to my eyes. Poor little urchin. Biking the cobbled streets in the rain. Touching his forelock. Knowing his place.

DAN: I don't know about touching my forelock. I used to put two fingers up to them when they weren't looking.

DOROTHY: Oh, good for you, Oliver Twist!

Dan throws himself playfully at Dorothy.

DAN: Yes. I wanted more - more - more!

DOROTHY: Watch it you fool! The fool.

Dan kisses Dorothy. The record ends, making a scratching noise. Dan gets up and takes off the needle. He sorts through a selection of records.

DAN: What would you like to hear? Tauber, Caruso, Clara Butt?

DOROTHY: Gracie Fields.

DAN: Gracie Fields? I didn't know you liked her.

DOROTHY: Sometimes. She makes me laugh.

She uses a teatowel for a headscarf and sings:

"The biggest aspidistra in the world".

DAN: *Sings*: "Sally! Sally! Pride of our alley". She makes me sick.

DOROTHY: You need to broaden your taste. You're far too serious, musically.

DAN: Right. Gracie it is, then.

Dan winds up the gramophone and puts on the record, "Wish Me Luck As You Wave Me Goodbye".

DOROTHY: No, not that one. I don't like that one.

Dan turns over the record to: "Let's All Go Posh", by Gracie Fields.

DAN: "Let's All Go Posh". Is that better?

DOROTHY: Most appropriate, I think.

They listen for a few seconds.

DAN: So, you think I'm too serious?

DOROTHY: Musically, yes.

DAN: Only musically?

DOROTHY: You're funny most of the time.

DAN: Most of the time?

DOROTHY: Sometimes you take yourself a bit too seriously.

DAN: Do I?

DOROTHY: Sometimes you try too hard to be amusing.

DAN: I can't win, can I?

DOROTHY: You should just relax and be yourself. Mummy and Daddy think you're smashing.

DAN: Smashing. *Imitating her.*

DOROTHY: Fool?

She offers him a dish.

DAN: I told you, don't be so personal. Ugh! This is awful.

DOROTHY: Maybe you'd like it better if I sprinkled some *She imitates his accent*: "little chocolate bits" on it. Here, have some cake instead.

DAN: Thank you.

Dan lies back.

DAN: I once cycled all the way from Hull to Pwllheli.

DOROTHY: Pwllheli. *She corrects his pronunciation.*

DAN: Whatever. Anyway, how come you're so good at pronouncing all these unpronounceable Welsh names?

DOROTHY: When you come to live among the natives, it pays to know the lingo.

DAN: Do you miss London?

DOROTHY: Not much. I certainly don't miss the bombing. Do you miss Hull?

DAN: Hull. *He corrects her pronunciation.*

DOROTHY: Hull.

DAN: I miss my family. I miss my sister, Joan and Mam and Dad. Our Eva's got a bairn now.

DOROTHY: A bairn?

DAN: A kid. I'm an uncle.

DOROTHY: Well done. What about all your pals at university?

DAN: University College. It isn't grand enough to be called a university. Not many "dreaming spires".

DOROTHY: Well, do you miss them? And what about the women?

DAN: The men outnumbered the women four to one. I didn't stand much of a chance.

DOROTHY: I don't believe that. A good looking man about town, like yourself. If I'd have been there, I'd have been after you like a shot. And what about all those parties?

DAN: I was too busy.

DOROTHY: A bit of a swot, eh?

DAN: I was too busy writing. I didn't put in any work for my degree. I only just managed to scrape through with a 2.1. It wasn't my idea of education. The place was just a factory for churning out teaching fodder for the elementary schools.

DOROTHY: I thought you loved teaching.

DAN: I want to be a writer. But one has to make a living.

DOROTHY: I'd love to read some of your work.

The record comes to an end.

DAN: Shall I put on some more Gracie?

DOROTHY: No, she can be a bit too jolly sometimes. Dan, Daddy's got this idea for a new venture after the war. He's going to open a chain of holiday camps around the country.

DAN: Holiday camps?

DOROTHY: Yes. I suppose he got the idea from his friend, Billy Butlin. You remember, you met him once at our house.

DAN: Well?

DOROTHY: Well, Daddy likes you so much, I'm sure he'd give you a job.

DAN: And what would I do, be a Red Coat or something? Wakey! Wakey! Campers. I can't sing and I only know a couple of jokes.

DOROTHY: No, silly, you'd help to run them. It would mean you'd have plenty of time for your writing.

DAN: Holiday camps! Pap for the masses. Bread and circuses. I don't think I'd be much good at that game.

DOROTHY: You are a snob sometimes. Daddy's only giving people what they want.

DAN: Oh? And what's that?

DOROTHY: A bit of happiness.

DAN: Happiness? You mean that by going for a week to one of your Daddy's camps people are going to find happiness?

DOROTHY: It's a chance to get away from it all. Have a break from reality.

DAN: If people faced up to reality they'd be a hell of a sight better off than singing "I do like to be beside the seaside" with hundreds of other poor, ignorant sods all pretending to have a good time.

DOROTHY: What's wrong with having a good time? Working class people, the "ignorant sods" as you call them, need to relax in their own way, just as much as...

DAN: What the hell are you talking about? Ignorance has got nothing to do with class. That's not what I'm saying. Back in the mess with my fellow officers, most of whom come from public schools by the way, we talk mindless smut all the time. If the radio is on and Mozart or Beethoven comes on there's an almighty shout goes up: "Turn it off!" It's more than ignorance. It's a hatred of beauty and grace and truth. And these are the leaders who are fighting for our culture. Oh, I'm sorry. You know what I'm like when I get on my soapbox. I'll put another record on, shall I?

DOROTHY: The thing is, reality is too painful for most people. That's why they prefer holiday camps.

DAN: Being in the army is a bit like being in a holiday camp.

DOROTHY: Don't let Daddy hear you say that.

DAN: When I first joined up I was so miserable. I put it down to being away from home at first. Then I realised what was happening. They were taking my soul away from me - bit by bit - with their inhumanity and their coarseness. So, I put up my defences. I pretended I was one of the lads. I told dirty stories, cursed, I was hearty: "I do like to be beside the seaside!" Meanwhile, my soul crouched behind the defences and tried to get by.

DOROTHY: I wish you'd let me get through those defences.

DAN: Dorothy, you wouldn't like what you found there.

He puts on a record: "Smile When You Say Goodbye", by Gracie Fields.

DAN: Come on let's dance.

They dance, Dan trying hard to keep in step.

DAN: Sorry! Two left feet.

DOROTHY: You haven't had much practice, have you?

DAN: No. Never had time for this sort of thing.

DOROTHY: Too busy writing.

DAN: Right.

DOROTHY: It's never too late to learn. Here, put your arm around here and you lead, I'll follow.

They do a few steps.

DAN: Is that better?

DOROTHY: A bit, but hold me tighter, so I'll know what you're going to do next.

They dance.

DOROTHY: That's much better.

DAN: I'm getting the hang of this.

DOROTHY: You're not exactly Fred Astaire, but you'll do.

DAN: Not exactly Fred Astaire, eh?

He grabs Dorothy and they go into an energetic parody of an Astaire/Rogers routine.

DAN: How am I doing, Ginger?

DOROTHY: Swell, Fred!

As the record and the dance routine end, Dan kisses Dorothy. He falls onto the rug, pulling Dorothy down with him.

DAN: See, I'm a quick learner.

DOROTHY: That's because you've got such a good teacher.

DAN: Yes, but the pupil's got to want to learn. You can lead a horse to water...

A cycle bell is heard offstage.

BOY: *Offstage.* Lieutenant Billany.

A telegram boy enters pushing a bike.

BOY: I'm looking for Lieutenant Billany. They told me up at the house that I'd find him down here.

DAN: I'm Lieutenant Billany.

BOY: Telegram for you, sir.

Dan signs for it and takes it. Dorothy stands looking as Dan reads the telegram. He hands it to Dorothy, grabs his battledress and Officer's cap and stick and exits. Dorothy reads the telegram as the voice of Joan is heard on the PA system.

JOAN: Lieutenant Dan Billany. Number 163 Officer Cadet Training Unit, Pwllheli, North Wales. Bombed out. Stop. Mother and Dad in hospital. Stop. Come quickly. Stop. Joan.

Dorothy exits, taking the basket and blanket with her. The stage darkens and the SFX of an air-raid can be heard. *As the lights come up we hear the SFX of the seaside. Joan is sitting on the rostrum. She is dressed in a warm coat and writes occasionally in a pad as she speaks.

JOAN: It's cold today, but I just had to come out here so I could see the sea and feel the wind and try to get my thoughts together. I'm sitting on that little cliff near the caravans and huts at Hornsea. Do you remember? Mam and Dad used to bring us here for our day out every Whitsuntide. You let me bury you up to the neck in the sand.

---

*see appendix A for Hill Street Theatre alternative.

She pauses.

For a moment then I had this picture in my mind of Mam, buried up to her neck in the ruins of our house. I still have nightmares. My hearing is coming back and the cuts and bruises have healed, but I can't get over seeing our Mam and Dad trapped in the blackness and wet in all that rubble. Our lovely new house flattened to the ground. Do you know, I'd just painted the scullery floor with red liquid lino floor paint. It shone so bright.

When I think of how close we once all were and now me in Cottingham, Mam and Dad in hospital in Leeds, Eva with her youngster in Lincolnshire and you ready to go abroad to God knows where: everything smashed and broken and scattered.

The new illustrations for The Magic Door are better than my old drawings, I think. I'm sure you'll love them. The publishers are very pleased. I keep pushing them for a publishing date. They're talking about early '42 now.

I met a colleague of yours from Hall Road School last week. Mr. Twiddy. He says that they'll be using extracts from The Magic Door to stimulate the kids when it's finished. So, new school, new ideas - you certainly left your mark, Dan. I'm sure they'll welcome you back with open arms when things get back to normal. If they ever do. Things will never be the same. But I want us all to be together again. I want you to come back to us safe and sound and then we can try and forget the terrible things that have happened.

I went back with Ken to Lakeside Grove to have another look through the rubble. Guess what we found? Three of your records, still intact! The Hallelujah Chorus, Bach's Jesu Joy of Man's Desiring and ...

The lights cross fade as Joan exits. Exit

DAN: ... One Fine Day.

Dan whistles a few bars.

DAN: That was the other record that Joan found in the rubble.

DAVID: It's amazing that it survived all that.

DAN: Mam nearly died. When I saw her in the hospital, she was swathed in bandages. All the skin from just above her eyes had been sliced off and peeled back by the force of the explosion, hair and everything, right back to the top of her head. Everything ended for me then. Seeing the people I loved crushed and destroyed like that. I went to look at the pile of bricks that had been our home and it was like my whole life lay there, shattered by that mine that came floating down from the sky under its silken parachute. Nothing to go back to. Everything in ruins.

There is a pause as Dan pulls the chair up to the stove and sits. He goes into a coughing spasm.

DAVID: What about Dorothy?

DAN: She joined the WRAC. We'll always be friends. We have a lot in common.

DAVID: That sounds like the basis for a good relationship.

DAN: That's what I kept telling myself. But when I held her I knew. She was too soft - too smooth. She didn't have the strength. The strength of a man. I'll never be able to love her, David.

DAVID: You haven't given yourself much of a chance, have you?

DAN: It's never too late to learn?

Dan laughs. He takes two cigarettes from a pack.

That was one of Dorothy's favourite sayings.

DAVID: And she was right.

DAN: No. Until the last weeks in the camp at Fontanellato I thought that too. I thought that I had a duty to everybody, including myself. I'd worked out that if I was ever going to stop feeling like a kid and grow up, I'd have to have the courage to give myself to a woman. I'd have to get married. But, the self is too precious to give to somebody you don't truly love. That would be a lie. You know, I'd actually kidded myself that it would be OK. I had this dream where you got married to my sister, Joan and I got married to Dorothy and everybody lived happily ever after. I even wrote to Joan telling her how handsome and kind and strong you were, and how she must marry you. You were the ideal man.

Dan lights the two cigarettes.

DAVID: You promised that we would have no more of this.

DAN: Don't you see, David? All that uncertainty and searching has led me here. To this little hut on the side of an Italian mountain. I didn't know what I needed to be happy - until now. I feel like I've been walking up this mountain all my life. I could never see where the road was leading. But now I see that it's been taking me in just one direction - to you. And there is no going back.

Dan offers David the lighted cigarette. David faces Dan for a long moment in a state of anger and impotence. He knocks the cigarette out of Dan's hand. Dan starts a coughing spasm. David looks at him.

DAVID: Go to hell!

David exits knocking the utensils off the table as he does so.

DAN: David.

The lights fade.

End of Act 1

Act II

Dan is sitting motionless near the stove with a spotlight on him. The rest of the stage is in darkness for a few moments. When the lights come up on this area we see that a table and chairs have been set below the rostrum. Henry is standing on the rostrum arms behind his back, leaning into the wind, looking into the audience with a fierce stare. He breaks his stance to pace around the rostrum. Alan is reclining elegantly in one of the chairs watching Henry. Bill enters with a tray and goes to the table. Bill, Henry and Alan are dressed in POW clothes.

BILL: Your tea, signore. And your manservant, signore Bunter, says he will be with you as soon as he has finished starching your shirts.

ALAN: Thank you.

Alan tips him and he bows.

BILL: Grazie mille, signore.

ALAN: Tell me, signore, who is that rather fearful looking chap striding about up there?

BILL: Oh, that is Capitano Henry, signore. He always takes his walk at this time of day.

ALAN: Henry? Are you sure his name's Henry? He bears a striking resemblance to the famous Captain Hornblower: hero of the English and scourge of the French.

Bill shrugs and exits. Alan gets up and goes over to the rostrum with his tea.

ALAN: *To Henry.* 'Morning, Henry.

Henry stops pacing and comes to the edge of the rostrum.

HENRY: Did you address me, Sir?

ALAN: As a matter of fact, I rather think I did.

HENRY: How dare you, Sir? I have given strict instructions that I should not be disturbed when I am pacing. Who the hell are you?

ALAN: I fear we have not been introduced, Captain. My name is Matsen, Alan Matsen. At your service, Sir.

HENRY: Strange, you bear a striking resemblance to that damn fop, Lord Peter Wimsey. What are you doing on my ship, Sir?

ALAN: I beg your pardon, Captain, but this is a cafe and I am waiting for a lady friend of mine.

HENRY: Women are not allowed on my ship, Sir. I'll have you flogged for this. Get below, damn you.

Henry continues his pacing. Alan returns to his seat.

Mr. Bush, take her half a point into the wind and close-haul the halyards. I don't like the look of that weather.

ALAN: Unreasonable fellow. Still, it takes all kinds I suppose.

Dorothy enters dressed as she was in Act 1.

DOROTHY: I'm sorry I'm so late, Darling. The traffic in Bond Street was simply awful. It took ages to get a taxi.

ALAN: Well, you're here now. Can I get you anything?

DOROTHY: I'd love some gooseberry fool, I think.

Bill enters.

ALAN: Gooseberry fool for the lady, per favore.

DOROTHY: With little chocolate bits on top.

BILL: Mi scusa, signorina?

DOROTHY: Come si dici in italiano? Ah, con vermicelli.

BILL: Si, naturalmente, signorina.

DOROTHY: You look exquisite today, darling. Your tie is a miracle of good taste.

ALAN: I can't take all the credit for that, my dear. Bunter looks after me so well.

David enters.

DOROTHY: Take a discreet look over there, darling. With that lazy grace of form and the cat-like swiftness of his movements, not to mention the engaging smile and the bantering ironic light in his eye, that can only be...

ALAN: David. David Dowie!

DOROTHY: Oh, really? He bears a striking resemblance to Simon Templar, The Saint.

David bounds quickly over to sit opposite Alan. They look at each other. Alan raises an enigmatic eyebrow, David lets a bantering smile play over his lips.

ALAN: Well, David.

DAVID: Well, Alan.

ALAN: You know David, Dorothy?

DOROTHY: We've never met, but Alan has told me so much about you, I feel I know you quite intimately already.

DAVID: Really?

He kisses Dorothy on the neck.

DAVID: I do beg your pardon, Old Boy. But whenever I see a pretty woman, I get carried away.

ALAN: Not at all, Old Man. Miss Warner and I will never be anything but good friends. But tell me, why are you here?

DAVID: I think you know that as well as I do Alan, Miss Warner...

DOROTHY: Please, call me Dorothy.

They exchange a look.

DAVID: ...Dorothy is in great danger.

DOROTHY: Danger?

ALAN: Yes, my dear. I tried to keep it from you, but you see, it's to do with your father's business.

DOROTHY: Daddy's holiday camps?

DAVID: Yes. the French...

ALAN: ...are trying to kidnap you...

DAVID: ...for the plans.

ALAN: Plans which could affect...

DAVID: ...the lives...

ALAN: ...of millions of people.

DAVID: Yes, that's why the Captain's here.

ALAN: Ah! I wondered about that.

DAVID: And that's why I'm here.

ALAN: That's why we're all here. To protect you, my dear.

DAVID: So you needn't worry your pretty little head anymore.

David gives Dorothy a long hard kiss.

DAVID: I'm sorry but I couldn't resist that.

DOROTHY: That's all right, David. I can see that you are easily aroused. I'll leave you for a while so that you can compose yourself. You men need to talk business.

She gets up and stands smoking a cigarette DS of the rostrum.

DAVID: Damn fine woman.

ALAN: Oh, God, yes. The best.

DAVID: But you and her...?

ALAN: Oh, God, no. I told you...

DAVID: Ah, yes. Good friends.

ALAN: I'm so glad that we're working together on this case, David. You know I admire you tremendously.

DAVID: The feeling is mutual, Old Boy.

ALAN: I've heard such fantastic things about you. You're a real hero. You have almost supernatural powers. The Robin Hood of the twentieth century. And there's something about the way your smile sets tiny wrinkles twinkling at your eye corners. Yet the eyes themselves, so direct and steel blue, have no share in the smile.

DAVID: I must confess you're a bit of a hero to me, Old Man.

David places his hand on Alan's knee.

ALAN: Am I really?

DAVID: Yes. A well known book collector, man about town, upholder of the law both here and abroad, distinguished criminologist - and you have such finely chiselled features, with just a hint of puckish humour.

ALAN: We heroes should stick together, don't you know.

They move their heads slowly towards each other, as if to kiss on the lips. At the very last moment, they are interrupted by a shout.

HENRY: Woman on board!

Dorothy has climbed onto the rostrum. Henry grabs Dorothy.

HENRY: How dare you disobey my orders, ma'am! My God, you remind me of Lady Barbara.

Henry kisses Dorothy hard on the mouth.

DAVID: What do you think you're doing, you old sea-dog? That's no way to treat a lady. Let her go, damn you.

David bounds towards Henry. Without looking or stopping what he is doing, Henry pulls out a pistol and shoots David. David stops dead in his tracks and falls to the floor, fatally wounded.

DAN, ALAN and DOROTHY *together*:
David!

Snap blackout. Dorothy, Alan, Henry and David exit. The spotlight brightens on Dan. After a few moments, the general lighting for the hut is brought up. Dan gets up and looks around the hut. He goes to the cupboard and sorts through the contents. He finds a tin of sardines and at the back of the cupboard a bottle of wine. He blows the dust off the bottle and opens it. He drinks straight from the bottle. As he does so the door opens. David is standing there, carrying a bundle of wood. He goes to the stove and starts to re-kindle the fire. There is a pause before Dan speaks.

DAN: You came back.

David doesn't answer and concentrates on the stove.

DAN: I thought you'd gone.

DAVID: I went for a walk.

DAN: A walk?

DAVID: Down the mountain. I got as far as the road. There's a sign post.

DAN: To where?

DAVID: I don't know. It seems there's more to escaping than getting outside the wire. You have to know where you're going.

Dan sits by the stove and takes out two cigarettes.

DAVID: When I opened the door just now, I half hoped this place would be empty.

Dan lights the cigarettes and gives one to David.

DAN: But I'm still here.
Some servants and some soldiers draw no pay,
Nor come when called, nor go when sent away.

DAVID: No. No more hiding behind words.

Dan grins.

DAVID: Look if we're ever going to get out of - this. *He indicates himself and Dan.* If we're ever going to sort this thing out between us, we have to speak the same language.

DAN: Speak the same language? I've always been truthful to you. We wrote a book together, remember.

DAVID: If that book ever gets published the librarians are going to have a hell of a job deciding which shelf to stick it on.

DAN: What do you mean?

DAVID: Fiction or non-fiction. The book is supposed to be a record of our life in the camps, but it's more like a novel - all that bloody psychology. All those characters you made up.

DAN: I made a few names up that's all. Everything else was real enough. Facts don't tell the whole story. It's what goes on inside people that counts. What happens between them when fate sticks them together in a hell hole like Capua or Fontanellato. Anyway, we were real enough.

DAVID: We should never have written the damn thing.

DAN: But we did.

DAVID: All that stuff about our thoughts and feelings.

DAN:	But that's what we experienced.
DAVID:	I don't like the idea of the world seeing our dirty washing.
DAN:	It's too late to get cold feet now. The book's finished.
DAVID:	It's not published.
DAN:	It will be.
DAVID:	Do I have a say in this too?
DAN:	Of course.
DAVID:	Well, maybe I don't want it publishing.
DAN:	Then what was the point in writing it?
DAVID:	I don't know. Therapy I suppose.
DAN:	You write something because you want other people to read and understand your thoughts.
DAVID:	Some thoughts are too private for other people to know about.
DAN:	Sometimes even the most private thoughts need to be shared.
DAN:	But some of that stuff that you make Alan say and do. People will never understand him. He's pure fiction.

DAN: He's the tragic hero.

A spot comes up on Alan Matsen who is sitting on the rostrum.

DAVID: He doesn't exist.

DAN: Doesn't he?

DAVID: You made him up. Put words into his mouth.

DAN: Alan is the real me: unhappy, insecure - a bit of a mess.

DAVID: The book would have been better off without him.

DAN: The book couldn't have been written without him. I don't know about him being a tragic hero, that's for others to decide. *(SFX - sounds of the prison camp)* But Alan exists alright.

General lighting comes up as Bill and Henry enter. They proceed with a game of Volley Ball US. David steps out of the hut and goes across and sits next to Alan. A spot remains on Dan, as he watches the action.

ALAN: I want to grow old with Auden. You see, his work changes with his personal growth and with the transformation of society. Auden believes that change is the essence of life, a fundamental truth. Tennyson said the same thing, "That men may rise on stepping stones/ Of their dead selves to higher things".

DAVID: Hey! Hang on. Don't go so fast, you're losing me.

ALAN: Sorry. I know I get carried away, but Auden says so much about the human experience. He's so modern.

Bill comes DS to retrieve the ball. He stands listening, then goes back US.

ALAN: "We need to love all since we are
Each a unique particular
That is no giant, god or dwarf,
But one odd human isomorph".

You see, Auden even uses science.

DAVID: Yes, I like that: "one odd human isomorph".

ALAN: He says so much about the way I feel. It's like I know him. I think he's wonderful.

DAVID: Hm, I can see that. You know, I've never had a man quoting poetry at me before.

ALAN: I don't make a habit of it. But, there are some people you feel close to right from the start. You can trust them. Oh, shit. It's so difficult to put some experiences into every day words. That's why we have poetry, I suppose, to make things clearer.

DAVID: Hm. Poetry doesn't make anything any clearer to me. But, I think I know what you mean. It's a sort of connection. Like when a beautiful, curving pass connects and you saw it coming in the bloke's eyes before he threw the ball.

Bill misses a volley by Henry.

BILL: Oh, yes! Nice one, Henry.

David retrieves the ball and throws it back US. He remains standing.

ALAN: Yes, that's it. Something like that.

Alan goes to David. He pulls a small parcel from his pocket.

ALAN: By the way, I got another parcel from home today.

DAVID: Oh, that's good. I'm still waiting for mine.

ALAN: There were two sets of underwear. I'd like you to have one.

DAVID: No. I couldn't accept that.

ALAN: Why not? I've got two sets, you've got none. It would be silly for you to be cold, when I've got enough for both of us.

DAVID: You've already given me cigarettes and food. I don't see what you get out of it.

ALAN: I like giving you things.

DAVID: It puts me under a bit of an obligation, though, doesn't it?

ALAN: No. Not at all. Don't feel like that about it, just accept it.

Bill and Henry come DS.

HENRY: Fancy a game, David?

BILL: Or are you too busy talking about bluebells to Alan?

HENRY: Come on. We'll take both of you on.

ALAN: No. Leave me out.

BILL: Alan prefers to wander lonely as a cloud among the bluebells.

ALAN: Daffodils.

BILL: Oh, sorry. I always thought it was bluebells.

Bill throws the ball to Alan. Alan drops it.

BILL: Oops! Butter fingers.

David picks up the ball.

DAVID: Come on, Alan. We'll take them on and thrash them.

ALAN: No. I'll let you down.

DAVID: No you won't. It's only a game.

David drags Alan CS and places him in position.

DAVID: You stand there, OK? You've watched us play before. You know what to do.

The game starts and Alan makes only a token effort to play. David plays for both of them. Bill and Henry quickly score as Alan trips, hopelessly missing the ball.

BILL: Trip over a bluebell, Alan? Or was it a pansy?

ALAN: *To David.* I told you.

HENRY: Come on. You're doing fine, Alan

David looks at Alan who is totally embarrassed.

DAVID: I think we'll give it a miss, if you don't mind. It's nearly time for the roll-call bell anyway.

HENRY: Yes, you're right. We ought to be making tracks too.

Bill and Henry go to exit. As they walk off, Bill sings:

BILL: Bluebells are bluebells,
Bluebells are blue.
Pansies are Pansies
But bluebells are blue.

Bill guffaws with laughter and Henry joins in. They exit, Bill still singing. David sits next to Alan on the rostrum.

ALAN: I'm sorry.

DAVID: What for?

ALAN: For letting you down.

DAVID: It's only a bloody game.

ALAN: I want you to respect me.

DAVID: What are you talking about? I do respect you. Just because you can't hit a bloody ball doesn't mean I don't respect you.

ALAN: I want them to respect me too. For your sake.

DAVID: Do they matter?

ALAN: No.

DAVID: Well, then.

Alan takes out the parcel again.

ALAN: Please take this.

DAVID: I've already said...

ALAN: Please.

DAVID: Oh, alright. If you insist.

ALAN: It's a thank you. Just to show how grateful I am.

DAVID: Grateful?

ALAN: For your being here. For being my friend.

DAVID: Alan, you should understand something. I'm here because I like being here. I enjoy talking to you. I like the feeling of being free to talk about things which I wouldn't dream of talking about to anyone else. So stop being so bloody grateful all the time.

David puts his arm around Alan's shoulders. Alan freezes with surprise. A bell rings off stage.

DAVID: That's the roll-call bell.

David gets up.

DAVID: Ready?

ALAN: You go. I'll be along in a minute.

DAVID: Don't keep the comandante waiting. You know how excited he gets if he doesn't see all our smiling faces on parade. Hey, cheer up. It's the specialite de la maison tonight - macaroni soup. I think someone ought to tell the comandante we can have too much of a good thing, don't you?

The SFX of the prison camp are brought up and merge with the distant sound of a voice singing quietly "Bluebells are bluebells...". David steps into the hut leaving Alan on the rostrum. A spot remains on Alan during the following scene.

DAN: Poor Alan. What an effect you had on him. The poor sod was traumatised and all because you put your arm around him.

DAVID: In a perfectly straightforward and natural way.

DAN: He didn't see it like that. His heart was thumping so hard he was afraid you'd hear it.

DAVID: He forced himself on me, just like he forced his gifts on me.

DAN: Did he, David?

Dan coughs and the pain from his shoulder overwhelms him.

DAVID: It was like having a dog. A dog that followed me around everywhere. What could I do?

DAN: You could have given it a biscuit.

DAVID: It used to give me biscuits and cigarettes and clothes.

DAN: You could have kicked it away, called it a bad dog.

DAVID: I tried that. It always crawled back.

DAN: You should have kicked harder.

DAVID: No. I didn't want to hurt him. I wanted him as a friend. But I didn't want those sad, pleading eyes looking forlornly up at me all the time.

The lighting increases on Alan who is now lying on the rostrum with a blanket over him. Another blanket has been placed a short distance away for David's bunk. David walks across and sits on the edge of the rostrum.

ALAN: I've been waiting for you.

David gets into his bunk.

ALAN: I need to talk to you.

David turns away from Alan.

DAVID: I don't want to talk. Go to sleep.

ALAN: David, please. Why did you spend all day avoiding me?

DAVID: Because I chose to. Now go to sleep, you'll wake the others.

ALAN: Why do you resent me? Why do you shut yourself away from me? I thought we understood each other.

DAVID: This is damned silly.

ALAN: You enjoyed being with me, you said. You enjoyed talking freely, about anything, you said. Then you go away and it's like we never even talked.

DAVID: This is stupid.

ALAN: Why are you shutting me out, David?

DAVID: Keep your voice down.

ALAN: Do you remember that day in the desert when we were captured?

DAVID: What about it?

ALAN: Remember how afterwards we talked about how we felt?

DAVID: Yes.

ALAN: Scared, ashamed, guilty, desperate, alone. That's how I'm feeling now - and worse. I'm so unhappy.

DAVID: I didn't take you prisoner. You can't hold me responsible for your unhappiness.

ALAN: I can't help myself.

DAVID: It's time that you did.

ALAN: Some nights I can't sleep. I just lie here listening to you breathe.

DAVID: Don't you think that we have enough to put up with just being in this place without making things ten times worse with all this?

ALAN: But you don't understand. I'm not just in a prison camp. I'm in solitary confinement. I have been for twenty seven years.

DAVID: What do you want from me?

ALAN: I need to break out of here. I need somebody to help me get out of this cage. I want you to help me to find the key before I go mad.

No, don't turn away. I haven't finished. Maybe you're afraid of what you might find inside. But there's no monster there. Just a pathetic little animal who's been caged for too long.

I want to tell you... I have to tell you. I love you.

David sits up and looks at Alan for a long moment. He then quietly folds down his blanket and walks away. He stands looking out SL.

DAVID: Another gift I didn't want. Until then I suppose I was flattered and a bit curious about what was happening to us. I'd allowed things to go on because it was a new experience that I rather enjoyed. But I wasn't in the least prepared for those three - little - words.

DAN: He was terribly hurt when you didn't respond. He was totally confused.

DAVID: His confusion was nothing compared to mine.

Henry enters and stands centre stage smoking a pipe. Alan is pacing near the rostrum. David is SL. The three areas are defined by separate lighting.

Alan and David speak the following lines together.

ALAN: I want to talk to you about David, Henry.

DAVID: I want to talk to you about Alan, Henry.

HENRY: Oh, yes?

ALAN: You know him pretty well.

DAVID: You know him pretty well.

HENRY: Yes.

ALAN: This is very difficult, but I hope you might understand.

DAVID: This is very difficult, but I hope you might understand.

HENRY: I'll try.

ALAN: He's been making me very unhappy lately.

DAVID: He's been getting on my nerves lately.

HENRY: Any particular reason?

ALAN: I feel as though I want something from him, but I don't know what.

DAVID: He wants something from me, but I don't know what.

HENRY: Have you talked to him about it?

ALAN: I can't talk to him about it.

DAVID: I don't want to talk to him about it.

ALAN: I'm afraid.

DAVID: I'm scared.

HENRY: Well, you have to face up to this thing, whatever it is. What exactly are you trying to tell me, old boy?

ALAN: I...I'm...I'm very...fond of him.

DAVID: He...he's ...he's very...fond of me.

HENRY: Well, I'm very fond of you.

ALAN: No. No. I love him.

DAVID: No. No. He loves me.

HENRY: Look here, Old Man. Have you tried plenty of exercise and cold showers? That usually does the trick.

Henry exits, leaving Alan and David in their lighting areas SR and SL.

ALAN: All I want is for him to see me as I really am. I want to take off the mask and stop acting.

I want to feel close to him. To touch him. That's not unnatural, is it?

DAVID: Love? I don't understand that word. I don't trust it, especially coming from him. It's only natural, isn't it?

Alan turns to look at David. David turns his head towards Alan. Snap blackout on David's lighting area. Alan sits on the rostrum. As the lights come up on the hut we see David with Dan.

DAN: He took Henry's advice to heart, but the cold showers didn't work. They just shrivelled everything up for a while. But you got plenty of exercise - trying to run away from him.

Dan nods towards Alan who is walking around the edge of the rostrum.

DAVID: Only, of course, I couldn't.

He puts a piece of wood on the stove.

That's the last bit of wood.

Alan lies on his back on the rostrum. Dan moves to the edge of the hut area and looks at him.

DAN: He used to lie on his bunk for hours, eyes closed, making up endless conversations, where you would say the things he needed to hear.

He felt like he was in the giant's kitchen. Do you remember the story? The kids are all locked up, waiting to be eaten by the giant, one by one. And what do they do? They don't talk to each other.

                    They don't share their feelings and comfort each
                    other. They play games.

DAVID: Mostly that's the only thing to do.

Dan turns back to David.

DAN: Maybe for people like Henry and Bill, but not for
                you.

DAVID: Why am I so different?

DAN: Because you were brave enough to stop playing for
                a while. You looked around the kitchen, saw
                another scared kid and held his hand. But then for
                some reason you got scared again and went back to
                playing with the others.

Alan stands and moves downstage. He turns to look towards the hut. He turns away as general lighting comes up on the rostrum area which now represents the latrines at camp Fontanellato. David runs across to the rostrum as Bill and Henry enter. Bill and Henry race to the rostrum. David is first there and mimes dashing into a cubicle and slamming the door shut. He sits on the rostrum, using it as a toilet bowl. Bill beats Henry to the other cubicle and does the same as David. Henry waits outside, trying to contain himself. Alan is some distance away. He is miming shaving and washing himself.

HENRY: You bastard, Bill. I'm dying to use the bloody bog.
                That bloody stuff we ate last night has gone straight
                through me.

BILL: Hard shit, Henry. You'll just have to cross your
                legs and pray.

HENRY: Did you see that, Alan? Some bloody officer and gentleman, eh?

Alan smiles and continues with his ablutions.

BILL: Hey we've got a new khasi-artist. I haven't seen this one before. An intellectual too. It's in Latin. Can anyone translate? It says, "Non nobis solum, sed toti mundo nati".

HENRY: It probably means, "This is the place where the big nobs hang out".

BILL: No. "Mundi" means world, doesn't it? It must mean, "I've got the biggest nob in the world". Bragging bastard. Anything new in your trap, David?

DAVID: No. Same old stuff. "Do not stand upon this seat..."

DAVID/BILL/HENRY:
"...the crabs in here can jump six feet".

Bill, Henry and David all laugh.

HENRY: The old ones are still the best.

DAVID: Oh, wait. There's a new drawing. It looks like the biggest nob in the world.

BILL: Probably the same bloke. Got a nob fixation.

DAVID: Well, if it's as big as he makes out, I don't wonder.

HENRY: Come on, you chaps. Hurry up or I'm going to shit myself.

BILL: "Why are we waiting, Why are we waiting."

DAVID: Hey, someone's bored a hole through the wall again.

BILL: Where?

DAVID: Down there. To your - right.

BILL: Dirty bastard!

Bill and David bend down to look through the "hole". They move in unison and reach the "hole" together, spying each other's eyeball inches away. They both quickly recoil.

BILL: Bloody pervert. Who would want to do that?

HENRY: Never mind the bloody hole in the wall. Please. Haven't you finished yet?

David finishes. He tries to flush his toilet, but the plumbing doesn't work. He comes out.

DAVID: Sorry, Henry. It's broken again.

HENRY: That doesn't matter. Out of the way. Quick.

Henry goes into the cubicle and sits. David goes and stands beside Alan. He begins to wash and shave.

DAVID: 'Morning. Sleep well?

ALAN: OK. There's a new blade there if you want one.

DAVID: No thanks. This one is fine.

ALAN: Are you on the list for the walk this morning?

DAVID: Yes.

ALAN: So am I. Mind if I walk with you?

DAVID: No. That's OK.

ALAN: Maybe we can talk.

Bill comes out of the cubicle and stands on the other side of Alan.

BILL: God, Henry. You stink!

Henry is checking out the hole in the cubicle wall.

HENRY: You don't exactly smell like roses yourself, old boy.

BILL: Sod it. I'm not shaving today. What's the point anyway?

HENRY: CO's orders, old boy. Keeps up the old morale. Got to be ready for the big day.

BILL: Whenever that is.

DAVID: It can't be long now. It's over two weeks since our lads got into Sicily.

HENRY: One of the carabinieri told old Tom in room 22 that Mussolini resigned yesterday.

BILL: Just another bloody rumour. You know what the Italians are like - a load of bloody washerwomen.

Henry finishes his toilet and comes out of the cubicle

HENRY: I can't flush the damn thing. I'll have to get a bucket of water.

DAVID: Fancy a game this afternoon, Henry?

HENRY: Love to, old boy, but I'm practising for tonight.

BILL: Tonight?

HENRY: The concert. I'm playing the old violin.

BILL: Oh god. Do we have to listen to you squawking away all afternoon?

HENRY: Cheeky bugger. It's all in the name of art.

BILL: Art? Do you call that art? You and that Nancy boy who dresses up like a woman.

HENRY: Sid does a very good impersonation of Our Gracie.

BILL: Bloody pervert. I know what I'd do with 'em all.

Bill looks directly at Alan. Alan finishes his ablutions and goes outside. He sits and lights a cigarette.

BILL: I suppose we all have to go to this bloody concert?

HENRY: 'Fraid so, old boy. CO's orders. Good for...

BILL: ...morale. Yes I know.

David comes out and joins Alan. Alan offers David his half smoked cigarette.

DAVID: Thanks.

ALAN: Prego. I haven't seen much of you lately.

DAVID: You've seen me every day.

ALAN: About the other night.

DAVID: Forget it.

David moves away.

ALAN: That's just it I can't.

Bill comes out of the latrine.

BILL: Hey, look up there.

He points skywards.

DAVID: What?

BILL: There. Can't you see? Planes. Listen.

The faint drone of bombers is heard, gradually getting louder.

ALAN: There are dozens of them.

DAVID: Bloody hundreds.

Henry joins them.

BILL: Bombers.

HENRY: Heading south.

DAVID: They're ours.

The four of them break into loud cheering, jumping about and hugging each other. After some moments a klaxon is heard followed by a voice over a loud speaker.

VOICE: Attention! Attention! This is your Commanding Officer.

The four stand and listen as the drone of the bombers fades.

I have just received news that Mussolini has resigned. The new head of state, Marshal Badoglio, will be sworn in today. He says that he intends to restore the traditional constitution of Italy. I will expect you to be on parade at 1300 hours, when we will be able to let you have more information about further developments.

The four erupt with excitement. David hugs Alan. They move towards the area with the table and chairs. Bill jumps onto a chair.

BILL: *Singing.*
          When this bleeding war is over
          Oh, how happy we will be.
          When I get my Civvy clothes on,
          No more soldiering for me.

DAVID: No more bloody roll-calls

HENRY: No more listening to Bill's crap

DAVID: No more "Dopo domani"

BILL: No more smell of Henry's shit.

DAVID: *Spoken* No more macaroni soup.

BILL: No more bloody Wops.

DAVID: Sunday dinner.

HENRY: The wife.

BILL: The kids.

HENRY: A pint of best bitter.

They all savour the moment.

ALAN: Do you think things will be any different?

HENRY: I bloody hope not, old boy. There's nothing wrong with things as they were.

BILL: I tell you what I'm looking forward to most, getting behind the wheels of the old jam jar and going out onto the road again. I'm going to sell like hell. There's going to be lots of lovely cash about.

HENRY: Oh yes! But just think of those Sunday mornings. A game of golf, a few drinks at the nineteenth, then home for a bit of fore-play with the missus, eh?

ALAN: So, why have we been through all this?

HENRY: What?

ALAN: If nothing's going to change. If we're still going to have poverty and inequality and prejudice and hate.

HENRY: What? Well, yes, I see what you mean, old boy. Things were a bit tricky before the war, weren't they? But, once it's all over, it will be different, you'll see. Everybody will pull together. They say it'll be a land fit for heroes.

BILL: I should have thought it was obvious why we've been through all this. Even to someone like you. So we can all go back to a free country.

ALAN: Oh, we all march back to this land of the free and take up where we left off.

BILL: That's about it.

ALAN: None of us will be free.

BILL: What?

ALAN: Not while we're in our own little prisons.

HENRY: Own little prisons? What are you talking about, old man?

ALAN: The one's that we make for ourselves and each other

HENRY: Yes. I see.

ALAN: Real freedom is reaching out. Not being afraid of other people. Not being afraid of who you are.

Alan moves and looks directly at Bill.

HENRY: Look, old man, I don't feel very comfortable with this kind of conversation. I mean what's the point in it? It doesn't lead anywhere.

Bill moves and stands directly in front of Alan.

BILL: What Henry means is - these people who like reaching out, as you put it, well, he wouldn't want to reach out back to them. That sort are best kept at arms length.

ALAN: That sort?

BILL: The clever clever, left-wing, arty-farty sort.

ALAN: Oh, that sort.

BILL: They're the ones who hold us back. They stop us making the country what it should be.

ALAN: A land fit for heroes?

BILL: You'll be going back to being a teacher after the war, I suppose?

ALAN: I hope so.

BILL: I wouldn't let you teach my kids.

ALAN: Maybe it's a bit too late for them to learn.

BILL: Poisoning their minds.

Bill sticks his face into Alan's.

BILL: They're all the same. No respect. No loyalty.

Bill pushes Alan, taunting him.

HENRY: Steady on, old boy!

BILL: Agitators. Dole mongers. Riff-raff. Foreigners. Perverts.

Bill pushes Alan hard, knocking him to the floor. He makes a move to kick him as David steps in. David punches Bill hard and Bill staggers back.

BILL: One of them are you? I always thought so.

David grabs Bill by the neck.

DAVID: Keep your filthy mouth shut.

David pushes Bill roughly away. Bill stands rubbing his neck.

BILL: It's all well and good blaming Hitler. We could do with a bit of discipline in England. Keep the likes of you where they should be - in the gutter.

David grabs Bill again and is about to strike him when the klaxon sounds. They stand still as the voice of the Italian Comandante is heard.

COMANDANTE: Prigionieri. The gates are open. Go home. You are free.

Stirring music is played over the loud speaker. David and Bill stand looking at each other. Bill and Henry exit. David turns and helps Alan up. He holds Alan and they look at each other for a few moments. The lights fade as Alan exits and David returns to the hut area.

The lights come up on Dan and David in the hut.

DAN: Three little words. You are free. I love you. So hard to understand. Did you know that the ancient Greeks had six different words for love?

DAVID: How many words did they have for freedom?

DAN: Just one, I think.

Dan has a coughing spasm and holds his shoulder with the pain. David goes to look at the stove.

DAVID: It's gone out. Are you all right?

DAN: Will we ever be free while there are people like Bill?

DAVID: People like him have to be kept in their place.

DAN: You stuck up for me. You needn't have.

DAVID: I had to.

DAN: My hero. But why?

DAVID: Because I felt guilty.

DAN: Guilty? You?

DAVID: Yes.

DAN: I don't understand.

DAVID: Because I know how much you care for me. And in my own way I care for you. But I always denied it, to other people and to myself. I couldn't just accept it for what it was. Something that could do no harm to anybody. Something good in the middle of all this mess. And when it boils down to it, if we have to take sides, I am "that sort" too.

DAN: What would my sort do without your sort to stand up for us.

DAVID: We heroes should stick together.

DAN: I haven't made things easy.

DAVID: No. You always wanted more than I could give. And when you didn't get what you wanted you behaved like a kid.

DAN: That was Alan talking. He's gone now.

DAVID: You have to accept what I can give.

DAN: You can choose your own word for it.

DAVID: What?

DAN: From the six that the Greeks had. There's "Storge" - togetherness. "Pragma" - understanding. "Agape" - devotion.

DAVID: What about the others?

DAN: "Ludus" - adoration. "Mania" - obsession. And "Eros" - passion.

DAVID: I know which one I'll choose. For the time being.

David goes to the door and opens it.

DAVID: It's stopped snowing. It's nearly daylight. God, it's so beautiful.

He returns leaving the door open.

DAVID: Are you cold?

DAN: Bloody freezing.

David goes and sits behind Dan and holds him in his arms.

DAVID: Is that better?

DAN: Yes.

After a few moments.

DAN: We could go to Rome.

DAVID: Yes.

DAN: I'd never make it to the Allied Lines anyway.

DAVID: It's all downhill to Rome.

DAN: We could stay with Arturo's cousin. And then maybe after the war we'd get a chance to see all those beautiful things from the past.

DAVID: What's left of them.

A sound of a dog barking in the distance is heard.

DAVID: Listen. The Germans are up and about early.

DAN: The Pantheon has survived for nearly two thousand years. You can walk right inside it. There's this huge dome. It has a big hole in the middle and when you stand under it and look up, you can see the stars. The gods and goddesses have all disappeared, but it's still magnificent, so they say.

David gets up and goes to look through the door.

DAVID: I can just see them. There's a patrol up there on the other side of the ravine. They're coming this way. Alec and Arturo are not coming back. We have to see if we can make it on our own.

David helps Dan to his feet, but Dan's condition has seriously deteriorated. Dan sways and stumbles. David catches him and eases him down again.

DAVID: Maybe if you rest for just a bit longer, eh?

DAN: Yes.

David sits and resumes his position, holding Dan.

DAVID: Yes. We'll go to Rome.

DAN: Have you ever been to the opera?

DAVID: No.

DAN: We'll go.

DAVID: Yes.

DAN: Puccini. Madame Butterfly.

DAVID: I'll probably fall asleep. I warn you.

DAN: And then afterwards we'll go to a bar and get drunk and watch the world go by.

DAVID: Now that sounds more up my street.

DAN: That's weird.

DAVID: What?

DAN: I can see him over there.

DAVID: Who?

DAN: The Scott's Emulsion man.

DAVID: Who's he?

DAN: When I was sick as a kid, he used to creep into my bedroom. I'd be lying in bed in the dark and I'd hear the door slowly open. Then this figure would come into the room - just like he is there.

A big, gaunt man dressed in black oilskins and a sou'wester, smelling of seaweed and the ocean. He has a huge dead fish on his back. It's got a gaping mouth and cold, staring, fishy eyes

Oh, he's gone.

As the scene continues the light coming into the hut gets brighter.

DAN: You're right it is beautiful up here. Shall I tell you a Magic Door story?

DAVID: Yes.

DAN: It's about the Winged Boy and Time. The Winged Boy was the keeper of the Magic Door and Time was his father. Time used to let his son play tricks with him. That's how Mr. Billany and the boys all got through the door.

One day, one of the boys, Jimmy Corner I think it was, asked the Winged Boy what would happen if Time died.

"Daft question," said Squeak Morley. "How can Time die?"
"Well," said the Winged Boy, "I can't imagine it. I mean, he is my father after all."

"See!" grinned Squeak, pushing Jimmy Corner so that he lost his balance and nearly fell onto the Winged Boy.

"But, I've heard that it's possible," continued the Winged Boy, pushing Squeak back. "They say that perhaps when Time stops, eternity begins. And

Time's shop will be unlocked and you'll be given back all those things you thought you'd lost forever."

"But don't you know anything for certain?" asked White, who always liked to be sure of things.

A spot comes up on the boy, Jack Crossley who is standing on the rostrum. Jack Crossley is played by the same actor who plays the part of Alan Matsen. Jack continues reading from the book.

JACK: The Winged Boy shook his head. "I don't really understand politics. The old people talk about it. Hey, and I'm only a boy, even though I am a million years old. I've heard though, that there was someone who promised all sorts of wonderful things for you humans when Time is finished."

"What sort of things?" asked White. "Ten weeks holiday in the summer and loads of that home made beer that Squeak's Grannie makes?"

"More wonderful things than you could ever dream of," said the Winged Boy, smiling. "But, it's all right for you, when Time's gone I'm finished too." Jimmy Corner patted the Winged Boy on the shoulder. "Never mind, Wingy," he said consolingly, "after all, a million years is a long time."

"I bet you could do nearly everything in a million years." said Edward Grey.

The lights on the hut reach their maximum brightness and then there is a snap blackout in the hut area leaving a spot on Jack.

JACK: "What about the Magic Door?" asked Glover impatiently. "If we wait here talking, we'll never get through it."

"Yes, let's go." shouted the others, who were a little bored with all the talk to tell the truth, but they didn't want to hurt the Winged Boy's feelings by dashing off. In less than a minute they were on the other side of the door."

The lights fade on Jack. The lights come up on an empty stage. The hut has been swung around and the wall of the hut has been made to represent part of the wall of a foyer in a grand opera house. A red curtained doorway adjoins the wall at right angles. Soft red lights flood the stage. The SFX of the end of the aria, "One Fine Day" is heard. The aria comes to an end and there is the sound of applause. A bright light shines through the curtained doorway and the hubbub of audience noise is heard. David and Dan enter through the doorway. They are both dressed in dark suits, white shirts and ties. David takes out two cigarettes, lights them both and gives one to Dan.

DAN: Thanks.

DAVID: I enjoyed that.

DAN: I said you would. Just like a perfect pass - remember?

DAVID: How is it possible?

DAN: What?

DAVID: That there's still so much beauty around after all that's happened.

DAN: Because there's always someone there to pick the pieces from the rubble.

DAVID: Does your Magic Door work forward as well as back?

DAN: I don't know. I'd have to ask the Winged Boy. Why?

DAVID: I'd like to know if it will be a land fit for heroes.

DAN: I'm sure it will be.

DAVID: What about Bill and his like?

DAN: Oh yes. They'll still be there. No doubt about that and there'll be someone searching through the rubble that they make, picking up the pieces, polishing them and passing them on.

The SFX of the continuing opera are heard. Dan and David walk towards the curtained door. Dan pauses for a moment looking at David as he walks towards the door. The lighting dims, leaving just the light streaming through the doorway. The music stops.

DAN: Hey, David. Catch!

Dan throws an imaginary ball at David. David turns and reaches up and catches the ball. He smiles at Dan as the lights from the door snap to black.

END

APPENDIX A

Alternative scene with voice over:

The lights come up on Dan who is reading a well thumbed letter as we hear the voice of Joan.

VOICE-OVER: Dear Dan, I'm sitting on the cliffs near the caravans and huts at Hornsea. Do you remember? Mam and Dad used to bring us here every Whitsuntide. You used to let me bury you up to the neck in the sand.
II still have this picture in my mind of Mam buried up to her neck in the rubble of our lovely new house: everything smashed and broken.
I went back last week to look through the rubble and guess what I found? Three of your records, still intact! The Hallelujah Chorus, Bach's Jesu Joy of Man's Desiring and ...

DAN BILLANY

Born in 1913 into a poor Hull family, Dan Billany fought tenaciously to achieve his ambitions - a university degree, a job as a teacher and eventually fame as a best-selling author in Britain and the USA. *Dan Billany - Hull's lost hero*, is a carefully researched biography contrasting his adventures as a soldier, a prisoner of war and as a fugitive on the run in Italy with the inner turmoil of a man coming to terms with his homosexuality - a life cruelly cut short and enormous potential unrealised.

Dan Billany by Valerie A. Reeves and Valerie Showan
(Price £6.25)
ISBN 1 902039 01 7

www.hullcc.gov.uk/kingstonpress

Sales

City Information Service
Hull Central Library,
Albion Street,
Kingston upon Hull
HU1 3TF
UK
Telephone: +44 (0)1482 223344
Fax: +44 (0)1482 616896
E-mail: city.information@hullcc.gov.uk